To

_____

From

_____

365 Smiles a Year For Cat Lovers

FaithPoint™
PRESS

January 1

A cat makes all the difference between coming home to an empty house and coming home.

Unknown

January 2

Beware of people who dislike cats.
Irish Proverb

January 3

The cat is domestic only as far as suits its own ends; it will not be kennelled or harnessed nor suffer any dictation as to its goings out or comings in.

Saki (H. H. Munro)

January 4

Most beds sleep up to six cats. Ten cats without the owner.
Stephen Baker

January 5

Cats always seem so very wise, when staring with their half-closed eyes. Can they be thinking, "I'll be nice, and maybe she will feed me twice"?

Bette Midler

January 6

Among animals, cats are the top-hatted, frock-coated statesmen going about their affairs at their own pace. Dogs are the peasants, dutifully plodding behind their leaders.

Robert Stearns

January 7

What are the chances of a cat starting a nuclear war? Pretty negligible. It's not that they can't; they just know that there are much better things to do with one's time. Like lie in the sun and sleep. Or go exploring the world.

Unknown

January 8

It would be easier to write with a herd of buffalo in the room than even one cat; they . . . bite the end of the pen and walk on the typewriter keys.

Barbara Holland

January 9

These guys entertain, love, and are always there for me. I can never express how much I care for these three. All of my cats are adopted and all show their gratitude on a daily basis. I don't know where I would be without them.

Bill Goldberg

January 10

Cats have intercepted my footsteps at the ankle for so long that my gait, both at home and on tour, has been compared to that of a man wading through low surf.

Roy Blount Jr.

January 11

It is impossible to keep a straight face in the presence of one or more kittens.

Cynthia E. Varnado

January 12

Oh, cat; I'd say, or pray: be-ooootiful cat! Delicious cat! Exquisite cat! Satiny cat! Cat like a soft owl, cat with paws like moths, jeweled cat, miraculous cat!

Doris Lessing

January 13

Everyone knows cats are on a higher level of existence. These silly humans are just too big-headed to admit their inferiority.

Unknown

January 14

And God said, "Let the land produce living creatures according to their kinds: livestock, creatures that move along the ground, and wild animals, each according to its kind." …

Genesis 1:24

January 15

Watch a cat when it enters a room for the first time. It searches and smells about, it is not quiet for a moment, it trusts nothing until it has examined and made acquaintance with everything.

Jean Jacques Rousseau

January 16

But you must not think we allowed our kittens to behave badly. On the contrary, we tried all we could to teach them good manners.... "Well, I told you kittens are mischievous," Nanny said. "And some are more mischievous than others."

Ernest Nister

January 17

Are cats lazy? Well, more power to them if they are. Which one of us has not entertained the dream of doing just as he likes, when and how he likes, and as much as he likes?

Fernand Mery

January 18

Cats love one so much—more than they will allow. But they have so much wisdom they keep it to themselves.

Mary Wilkins

January 19

As a housepet, I'm overqualified.
Stephen Baker, speaking as a cat

January 20

Happy owner, happy cat. Indifferent owner, reclusive cat.

Chinese Proverb

January 21

Just think what a nicer world this would be if it were controlled by cats.

Unknown

January 22

Cats are smarter than dogs. You can't get eight cats to pull a sled through snow.

Jeff Valdez

January 23

No amount of time can erase the memory of a good cat, and no amount of masking tape can ever totally remove his fur from your couch.

Leo Dworken

January 24

Cat people are different, to the extent that they generally are not conformists. How could they be, with a cat running their lives?

Dr. Louis J. Camuti

January 25

Intelligence in the cat is underrated.
Louis Wain

January 26

Cat scan: When a cat checks out a yard for prey.

Richard L. Peterson

January 27

Cats understand our feelings. They don't care, but they understand.

Unknown

January 28

Cats don't like change without their consent.

Roger A. Caras

January 29

Cruel, but composed and bland,
Dumb, inscrutable and grand,
So Tiberius might have sat,
Had Tiberius been a cat.

Matthew Arnold

January 30

Don't think that I'm silly for liking it, I just happen to like the simple little things, and I love cats!

Michelle Gardner

January 31

Anyone who claims that a cat cannot give a dirty look either has never kept a cat or is singularly unobservant.

Maurice Burton

February 1

There is one way in which cats differ from all other animals and that is in the effect they have on human beings.

Patricia Dale-Green

February 2

Cats are possessed of a shy, retiring nature, cajoling, haughty, and capricious, difficult to fathom. They reveal themselves only to certain favored individuals, and are repelled by the faintest suggestion of insult or even by the most trifling deception.

Pierre Loti

February 3

If it were not for the recurring evidence of murder—the disemboweled rabbits, the headless flickers, the torn squirrels—we should forever imagine our cats to be simple pets whose highest ambition is to sleep in the best soft chair.

Robley Wilson Jr.

February 4

I wish I could write as mysterious as a cat.
Edgar Allan Poe

February 5

If you can remember how many cats you have, you don't have enough.

Unknown

February 6

Getting a cat is a greater commitment than getting married.

Paula Chwast

February 7

The cat is a dilettante in fur.

Theophile Gautier

February 8

We cannot, without becoming cats, perfectly understand the cat mind. The smart cat doesn't let on that he is.

St. George Mivart

February 9

If a cat does something, we call it instinct; if we do the same thing, for the same reason, we call it intelligence.

Will Cuppy

February 10

You can visualize a hundred cats. Beyond that, you can't. Two hundred, five hundred, it all looks the same.

Jack Wright

February 11

A cat's a cat and that's that.
American Proverb

February 12

A cat knows you are the key to his happiness... a man thinks he is.

Unknown

February 13

A cat is a lion to a mouse.
Albanian Proverb

February 14

Each cat I have reminds me of unconditional love. No matter what's going on in my professional life, I know that with my animals I'm always No. 1! If I'm with my cats, I'm also with God.

Wynonna

February 15

When we caress her, she stretches herself and arches her back; but this is because she feels an agreeable sensation, not because she takes a silly satisfaction, like the dog, in faithfully loving a thankless master.

Francois Rene de Chateaubriand

February 16

Cats are rather delicate creatures, and they are subject to a good many ailments, but I never heard of one who suffered from insomnia.

Joseph Wood Crutch

February 17

One reason we admire cats is for their proficiency in one-upmanship. They always seem to come out on top, no matter what they are doing, or pretend they do.

Barbara Webster

February 18

The wild animals honor me, the jackals and the owls, because I provide water in the desert and streams in the wasteland, to give drink to my people, my chosen, the people I formed for myself that they may proclaim my praise.

Isaiah 43:20-21

February 19

The cat: an animal that's so unpredictable, you can never tell in advance how it will ignore you the next time.

Evan Esar

February 20

After scolding one's cat, one looks into its face and is seized by the ugly suspicion that it understood every word. And has filed it for reference.

Charlotte Gray

February 21

I believe cats to be spirits come to earth. A cat, I am sure, could walk on a cloud without coming through.

Jules Verne

February 22

Each cat has a distinct purrsonality.
Richard L. Peterson

February 23

Artists like cats; soldiers like dogs.
Desmond Morris

February 24

The cat is the only animal without visible means of support who still manages to find a living in the city.

Carl van Vechten

February 25

What sort of philosophers are we who know absolutely nothing about the origin and destiny of cats?

Henry David Thoreau

February 26

Loneliness is comforted by the closeness and touch of fur to fur, skin to skin—or skin to fur.
Paul Gallico

February 27

It's funny how dogs and cats know the inside of folks better than other folks do, isn't it?

Eleanor H. Porter

February 28

If cats had wings, there would be no ducks in the lake.
Indian Proverb

February 29

Okay, cats will never bring you pictures they've drawn in school, but they may give you a dead mouse. What parent could resist that gift?

Terri L. Haney

March 1

A mouse in the paws is worth two in the pantry.
Louis Wain

March 2

Cats are intended to teach us that
not everything in nature
has a function.

Garrison Keilor

March 3

One of the most striking differences between a cat and a lie is that a cat has only nine lives.
Mark Twain

March 4

A cat knows exactly what you are,
and treats you accordingly.

Unknown

March 5

To anyone who has ever been owned by a cat, it will come as no surprise that there are all sorts of things about your cat you will never, as long as you live, forget. Not the least of these is the first sight of him or her.

Cleveland Amory

March 6

Experience is valuable in most human endeavors, but the problem of getting a cat down out of a tree is new every time it arises.

Francis Duffy

March 7

Cats are only human; they have their faults.

Kingsley Amis

March 8

It is a very inconvenient habit of kittens (Alice had once made the remark) that whatever you say to them, they always purr.

Lewis Carroll

March 9

Ignorant people think it's the noise which fighting cats make that is so aggravating, but it ain't so; it's the sickening grammar they use.

Mark Twain

March 10

All cats are possessed of a proud spirit, and the surest way to forfeit the esteem of a cat is to treat him as an inferior being.

Michael Joseph

March 11

> The trouble with a kitten is that eventually it becomes a cat!
>
> **Ogden Nash**

March 12

When my cats aren't happy, I'm not happy. Not because I care about their mood, but because I know they're just sitting there thinking up ways to get even.

Penny Ward Moser

March 13

"And to all the beasts of the earth and all the birds of the air and all the creatures that move on the ground—everything that has the breath of life in it—I give every green plant for food." And it was so.

Genesis 1:30

March 14

Authors like cats because they are such quiet, lovable, wise creatures, and cats like authors for the same reasons.

Robertson Davies

March 15

He seems the incarnation of everything soft and silky and velvety, without a sharp edge in his composition, a dreamer whose philosophy is sleep and let sleep.

Saki (H. H. Munro)

March 16

To bathe a cat takes brute force, perseverance, courage of conviction— and a cat. The last ingredient is usually hardest to come by.

Stephen Baker

March 17

Nothing's more playful than a young cat, nor more grave than an old one.
Thomas Fuller

March 18

For a man to truly understand rejection, he must first be ignored by a cat.
Unknown

March 19

Cats are connoisseurs of comfort.

James Herriot

March 20

A kitten is chiefly remarkable for rushing about like mad at nothing whatsoever, and generally stopping before it gets there.

Agnes Replier

March 21

Dynasties of cats, as numerous as the dynasties of the Pharaohs, succeed each other under my roof. The memory of the cats we have lost fades like the memory of men.

Theophile Gautier

March 22

If you're lucky enough to own a cat, consider yourself one of life's winners because when you have a cat around, you'll never be lonely; the sound of its purr will give you comfort, and as you hold it and pet it, stress will slip away.

Sharon Lundblad

March 23

Humans: No fur, no paws, no tail. They run away from mice. They never get enough sleep. How can you help but love such an absurd animal?

An anonymous cat on Homo sapiens

March 24

Avoid dogs whenever you can. Remember—cats are poetry in motion. Dogs are gibberish in neutral.

Unknown

March 25

A cat improves the garden wall in sunshine, and the hearth in foul weather.

Judith Merkle Riley

March 26

A man who carries a cat by the tail learns something he can learn in no other way.
Mark Twain

March 27

It is in the nature of cats to do a certain amount of unescorted roaming.

Adlai Stevenson

March 28

Cats' hearing apparatus is built to allow the human voice to easily go in one ear and out the other.

Stephen Baker

March 29

In a cat's eye, all things belong to cats.
English Proverb

March 30

I love my cats because I love my home, and little by little they become its visible soul.

Jean Cocteau

March 31

There was an old bulldog named Caesar, Who went for a cat just to tease her; but she spat and she spit, till the old bulldog quit. Now when poor Caesar sees her, he flees her.

Unknown

April 1

A poet's cat, sedate and grave as a poet well could wish to have.... Time, that spoils all things, will, I suppose, make her also a cat.... For no wisdom that she may gain by experience and reflection hereafter will compensate for the loss of her present hilarity.

William Cowper

April 2

Cats are autocrats of naked self-interest. They are both amoral and immoral, consciously breaking rules. Their "evil" look at such times is no human projection: The cat may be the only animal who savors the perverse or reflects upon it.

Camille Paglia

April 3

I will admit to feeling exceedingly proud when any cat has singled me out for notice; for, of course, every cat is really the most beautiful woman in the room. That is part of their deadly fascination.

E. V. Lucas

April 4

By associating with the cat, one only risks becoming richer.

Colette

April 5

They say a cat always lands on his feet, but they don't mention the pain.

Jim Davis, as Garfield the cat

April 6

In my experience, cats and beds seem to be a natural combination.

Dr. Louis J. Camuti

April 7

Every life should have nine cats.

Unknown

April 8

He who rides the tiger finds it difficult to dismount.

Chinese Proverb

April 9

The beautiful cat endures and endures.

Grave inscription from Thebes

April 10

One is never sure, watching two cats washing each other, whether it's affection, the taste, or a trial run for the jugular.

Helen Thomson

April 11

The playful kitten with its pretty little tigerish gambole is infinitely more amusing than half the people one is obliged to live with in the world.

Lady Sydney Morgan

April 12

"What is the appeal about cats?" he said kindly. "I've always wanted to know." "They don't care if you like them. They haven't the slightest notion of gratitude, and they never pretend. They take what you have to offer, and away they go."

Mavis Gallant

April 13

Cats don't bark and act brave when they see something small in fur or feathers—they kill it. Dogs tend to bravado. They're braggarts. In the great evolutionary drama, the dog is Sergeant Bilko, the cat is Rambo.

James Gorman

April 14

Blessed are those who love cats, for they shall never be lonely.

Unknown

April 15

How many are your works, O Lord! In wisdom you made them all; the earth is full of your creatures.

Psalm 104:24

April 16

Question: What about the way cats claw the upholstery?
Answer: Learn to like fringe!

Missy Dizick

April 17

Passion for place—there is no greater urge in feline nature.
Paul Annixter

April 18

If only cats grew into kittens.
R. Stern

April 19

A home without a cat—and a well-fed, well-petted and properly revered cat—may be a perfect home, perhaps, but how can it prove title?

Mark Twain

April 20

One of the ways in which cats show happiness is by sleeping.
Cleveland Amory

April 21

Dogs believe they are human. Cats believe they are God.

Unknown

April 22

There are few things in life more heartwarming than to be welcomed by a cat.

Tay Hohoff

April 23

In the beginning, God created man, but seeing him so feeble, He gave him the cat.
Warren Eckstein

April 24

I am in favor of animal rights as well as human rights. That is the way of a whole human being.

Abraham Lincoln

April 25

Subliminal kitty messages? "You are getting very sleepy" is not a command when said to a cat; it is an eternal truth.

Ari Ripkin

April 26

Of all the toys available, none is better designed than the owner himself. A large multipurpose plaything, its parts can be made to move in almost any direction. It comes completely assembled, and it makes a sound when you jump on it.

Stephen Baker

April 27

Cats can be cooperative when something feels good, which, to a cat, is the way everything is supposed to feel as much of the time as possible.

Roger A. Caras

April 28

Cats don't belong to people.
They belong to places.
Wright Morris

April 29

There is no snooze button on a cat who wants breakfast.

Unknown

April 30

Dogs eat. Cats dine.

Ann Taylor

May 1

Cats are just little hair factories.
James Davis, DVM

May 2

Never will you get a better
psychological subject
than a hungry cat.
Dr. Edward Lee Thorndike

May 3

When you come upon your cat, deep in meditation, staring thoughtfully at something that you can't see, just remember that your cat is, in fact, running the universe.

Bonni Elizabeth Hall (and Missycat)

May 4

Drowsing, they take the noble attitude of a great sphinx, who, in a desert land, sleeps always, dreaming dreams that have no end.

Charles Baudelaire

May 5

Cats have a curious effect on people. … There are people who cannot remain in the room with a cat—who feel instinctively the presence of a cat. … On the other hand, there are people who … will at once get up and fondle a cat immediately [when] they see it.

Arthur Ponsonby

May 6

A harmless, necessary cat.
William Shakespeare

May 7

These furry buggers are just deep, deep wells you throw all your emotions into.

Ernest Menual

May 8

I don't think it is so much the actual bath that most cats dislike; I think it's the fact that they have to spend a good part of the day putting their hair back in place.

Debbie Peterson

May 9

A dog, I have always said, is prose; a cat is a poem.

Jean Burden

May 10

I put down my book, THE MEANING OF ZEN, and see the cat smiling.... "Cat, I would lend you this book to study, but it appears you have already read it." She looks up and gives me her full gaze. "Don't be ridiculous," she purrs, "I wrote it."

Dilys Laing

May 11

I've never understood why women love cats. Cats are independent, they don't listen, ... they like to stay out all night, and when they're home they like to be left alone and sleep. In other words, every quality that women hate in a man, they love in a cat.

Jay Leno

May 12

The purity of a person's heart can be quickly measured by how they regard cats.

Unknown

May 13

As every cat owner knows,
nobody owns a cat.
Ellen Perry Berkeley

May 14

Cats instinctively know the precise moment their owners will awaken … then they awaken them ten minutes earlier.

Jim Davis

May 15

The cat is the only non-gregarious domestic animal.
Francis Galton

May 16

Everything I know I learned from my cat: When you're hungry, eat. When you're tired, nap in a sunbeam. When you go to the vet's, pee on your owner.

Gary Smith

May 17

My cat is concerned with the economy because his favorite kitty kibbles are over $1 a pound. He figures that's close to $15 a pound in cat currency.

Richard L. Peterson

May 18

Bring out every kind of living creature that is with you—the birds, the animals, and all the creatures that move along the ground—so they can multiply on the earth and be fruitful and increase in number upon it.

Genesis 8:17

May 19

A human may go for a stroll with a cat; he has to walk a dog. The cat leads the way, running ahead, tail high, making sure you understand the arrangement. If you should happen to get ahead, the cat will never allow you to think it is following you.

Robert Stearns

May 20

If we treated everyone we meet with the same affection we bestow upon our favorite cat, they, too, would purr.

Martin Buxbaum

May 21

Never underestimate the power of a purr.

Unknown

May 22

Cats exercise … a magic influence upon highly developed men of intellect. This is why these long-tailed Graces of the animal kingdom … have been the favorite animal of a Mohammed, Cardinal Richelieu, Crebillon, Rousseau, Wieland.

Leopold Von Sacher-Masoch

May 23

Quite obviously a cat trusts human beings, but she doesn't trust a cat because she knows her better than we do.

Karel Capek

May 24

How we behave toward cats here below determines our status in heaven. Women and cats will do as they please, and men and dogs should relax and get used to the idea.

Robert A. Heinlein

May 25

In the middle of a world that has always been a bit mad, the cat walks with confidence.

Roseanne Anderson

May 26

Owning a cat is like reading a good novel—just when you think you know the main character, she'll surprise you on the very next page.

Unknown

May 27

When a cat adopts you, there is nothing to be done about it except to put up with it until the wind changes.

T. S. Eliot

May 28

There's no need for a piece of sculpture in a home that has a cat.
Wesley Bates

May 29

I have studied many philosophers and many cats. The wisdom of cats is infinitely superior.

Hippolyte Taine

May 30

To please himself only, the cat purrs.
Irish Proverb

May 31

When I play with my cat, who knows if I am not a pastime for her more than she is for me?

Michel de Montaigne

June 1

Kittens are born with their eyes shut. They open them in about six days, take a look around, then close them again for the better part of their lives.

Stephen Baker

June 2

Of all God's creatures, there is only one that cannot be made slave of the leash. That one is the cat. If man could be crossed with the cat, it would improve the man, but it would deteriorate the cat.

Mark Twain

June 3

You are my cat, and I am your human.
Hilaire Belloc

June 4

Nine lives added to my one life makes a perfect 10.

Unknown

June 5

Friendship between cats can exist, but … in the same way that it can exist for a not very sociable man who … provok[es] others, and who, when asked why he does not have any friends, replies: "I would like to have them—but they are so ignoble!"

Paul Leyhausen

June 6

We should be careful to get out of an experience only the wisdom that is in it—and stop there; lest we be like the cat that sits down on a hot stove-lid. She will never sit down on a hot stove-lid again—… but also she will never sit down on a cold one anymore.

Mark Twain

June 7

In order to keep a true perspective of one's importance, everyone should have a dog that will worship him and a cat that will ignore him.

Dereke Bruce

June 8

I suspect that many an ailurophobe hates cats only because he feels they are better than he is—more honest, more secure, more loved, more whatever he is not.

Winifred Carriere

June 9

If I die before my cat, I want a little of my ashes put in his food, so I can live inside him.

Drew Barrymore

June 10

To respect the cat is the beginning of the aesthetic sense.

Erasmus Darwin

June 11

The cat has too much spirit to have no heart.

Ernest Menual

June 12

Dogs remember faces, cats places.
English Proverb

June 13

There are hundreds of good reasons
for having a cat, but all
you need is one.

Unknown

June 14

A dog will flatter you, but you have to flatter the cat.

George Mikes

June 15

Then God said to Noah . . .: "I now establish my covenant with you and with your descendants after you and with every living creature . . . on earth."

Genesis 9:8-10

June 16

Cats find malicious amusement in doing what they know they are not wanted to do, and … with an affectation of innocence that materially aggravates their deliberate offense.

Helen M. Winslow

June 17

Cats are masters of sublime hisssstrionics.

Katherine Palmer Peterson

June 18

Cats are glorious creatures who must on no accounts be underestimated.... Their eyes are fathomless depths of cat-world mysteries.

Lesley Anne Ivory

June 19

The cat is a creature of most refined and subtle perceptions naturally.

Roger A. Caras

June 20

In the night, all cats are gray.

Miguel de Cervantes

June 21

I think it would be great to be a cat! You come and go as you please. People always feed and pet you. They don't expect much of you. You can play with them, and when you've had enough, you go away. You can't ask for more than that.

Patricia McPherson

June 22

A cat is a very special friend who comes into your life. When it comes, it brings warmth, companionship, contentment, and love. Whether it's long-haired, short-haired, pedigreed, or "heinz" makes no difference.

Sharon Lundblad

June 23

Whether they be the musician cats in my band or the real cats of the world, they all got style.

Ray Charles

June 24

A dog is a man's best friend.
A cat is a cat's best friend.

Robert J. Vogel

June 25

I gave my cat a bath the other day. He just sat there. Actually, I think he enjoyed it. It wasn't very fun for me, though. The fur kind of stuck to my tongue.

Steve Martin

June 26

I love how independent and self-contained they are. I always feel it's an honor when one decides to let you into their world with a rub against the leg or a quick jump into your lap.

Tina Lifford

June 27

A cat can be trusted to purr when she is pleased, which is more than can be said for human beings.

William Ralph Inge

June 28

Which is more beautiful: feline movement or feline stillness?

Elizabeth Hamilton

June 29

The visionary chooses a cat; the man of concrete a dog. Hamlet must have kept a cat. Platonists, or cat lovers, include sailors, painters, poets, and pickpockets. Aristotelians, or dog lovers, include soldiers, football players, and burglars.

Unknown

June 30

Cats' names are more for human benefit. They give one a certain degree more confidence that the animal belongs to you.
Alan Ayckbourn

July 1

A cat's life is more important than art.
Alberto Giacometti, a sculptor

July 2

The cat is, above all things, a dramatist.

Margaret Benson

July 3

I think of a woman as something like myself.

Paul Gallico, translating from cat language

July 4

I care not for a man's religion whose dog or cat is not the better for it.

Abraham Lincoln

July 5

Prowling his own quiet backyard or asleep by the fire, he is still only a whisker away from the wilds.

Jean Burden

July 6

Perhaps cats and writers simply go together because the cat is the perfect companion for the solitary, sedentary artist.

Linda Sunshine

July 7

A cat assures its owner of good luck.
Chinese Proverb

July 8

Cats are dangerous companions for writers because cat watching is a near-perfect method of writing avoidance.
Dan Greenberg

July 9

The catlike man is one upon whom no tricks can be played with success.

Delphine Gay

July 10

Never play cat and mouse games if you're a mouse.
Don Addis

July 11

A cat is more intelligent than people believe, and can be taught any crime.

Mark Twain

July 12

I love cats. I even think we have one at home.
Edward Burlingame

July 13

Here lies a pretty cat: Its mistress, who never loved anyone, loved it madly; Why bother to say so? Everyone can see it.

Epitaph on tombstone of cat

July 14

If you take even one of a cat's nine lives, it will haunt you forever.

Unknown

July 15

Work—other people's work—is an intolerable idea to a cat. Can you picture cats herding sheep or agreeing to pull a cart? They will not inconvenience themselves to the slightest degree.

Dr. Louis J. Camuti

July 16

I think my favorite thing in the house has to be the cat... mainly because she's just like a big piece of noisy Velcro when you toss her at the sofa.

Michelle Argabrite

July 17

There stands before you, gray like all the other grays but one whom you won't confuse, having seen her once, with any other gray cat, she who rejects the names of queens ... and is called—as if she were the only one in the world—Cat.

Colette

July 18

The love of dress is very marked in this attractive animal. He is proud of the lustre of his coat, and cannot endure that a hair of it shall lie the wrong way.

Jules Champfleury

July 19

But buds will be roses, and kittens, cats—more's the pity!

Louisa May Alcott

July 20

A righteous man cares for the needs of his animal.

Proverbs 12:10a

July 21

If cats could talk, they wouldn't.
Nan Porter

July 22

When the cat and mouse agree,
the grocer is ruined.
Persian Proverb

July 23

Cats, by means of their whiskers, seem to possess something like an additional sense: These have, perhaps, some analogy to the antennae of moths and butterflies.

Rev. W. Bingley

July 24

Places to look: behind the books in the bookshelf, any cupboard with a gap too small for any cat to squeeze through, the top of anything sheer, under anything too low for a cat to squash under, and inside the piano.

Roseanne Ambrose-Brown

July 25

You can't own a cat. The best you can do is be partners.
Sir Harry Swanson

July 26

In ancient times, cats were worshipped as gods; they have not forgotten this.

Terry Pratchett

July 27

Cats are like greatness: Some people are born into cat-loving families, some achieve cats, and some have cats thrust upon them.

William H. A. Carr

July 28

When the rat laughs at the cat, there is a hole. The rat has not power to call the cat to account. The rat does not go to sleep in the cat's bed.

Unknown

July 29

I simply can't resist a cat, particularly a purring one. They are the cleanest, cunningest, and most intelligent things I know, outside of the girl you love, of course.

Mark Twain

July 30

If a dog jumps in your lap, it is because he is fond of you, but if a cat does the same thing, it is because your lap is warmer.

Alfred North Whitehead

July 31

Cats seem to go on the principle that it never does any harm to ask for what you want.

Joseph Wood Crutch

August 1

Cats regard people as warm-blooded furniture.
Jacquelyn Mitchard

August 2

Cats never feel threatened. They are genetically incapable of accepting that anyone could possibly dislike anything as perfect as a cat.
Kathy Young

August 3

Cat: a pygmy lion who loves mice, hates dogs, and patronizes human beings.

Unknown

August 4

There is, incidentally, no way of talking about cats that enables one to come off as a sane person.

Dan Greenberg

August 5

The ideal of calm exists in a sitting cat.

Jules Reynard

August 6

The kitten... never feels the necessity to do anything to justify its existence. It knows that it is beautiful and delightful, and it considers that a sufficient contribution to the general good.

Robertson Davies

August 7

The cat could very well be man's best friend but would never stoop to admitting it.

Doug Larson

August 8

If 'twere not for my cat and dog, I think I could not live.

Ebenezer Elliott

August 9

It is easy to understand why the rabble dislike cats. A cat is beautiful; it suggests ideas of luxury, cleanliness, voluptuous pleasures.

Charles Baudelaire

August 10

The real measure of a day's heat is the length of a sleeping cat.
Charles J. Brady

August 11

Essentially, you do not so much teach your cat as bribe him.

Lynn Hollyn

August 12

Take a cat, nourish it well with milk and tender meat, make it a couch of silk, but let it see a mouse along the wall, and it abandones milk and meat and all.

Geoffrey Chaucer

August 13

Maybe in the future we should ... ask ... presidential candidates ... where they stand on cats. Better still, we should demand to see the cats these candidates say they have raised, just to make sure we are not having the fur pulled over our eyes.

Gilbert Gude

August 14

A kitten is so flexible that she is almost double; the hind parts are equivalent to another kitten with which the forepart plays. She does not discover that her tail belongs to her until you tread on it.

Henry David Thoreau

August 15

A plate is distasteful to a cat, a newspaper still worse; they like to eat sticky pieces of meat sitting on a cushioned chair or a nice Persian rug. A cat must either have beauty and breeding, or it must have a profession.

Margaret Benson

August 16

In his castle
He is King
And I his vassal.

Mildred R. Howland

August 17

All you have to remember is Rule 1: When in doubt—wash.

Paul Gallico

August 18

I said something which gave you to think I hated cats. But gad, sir, I am one of the most fanatical cat lovers in the business. If you hate them, I may learn to hate you. If your allergies hate them, I will tolerate the situation to the best of my ability.

Raymond Chandler

August 19

Apparently, through scientific research, it has been determined that a cat's affection gland is stimulated by snoring, thus explaining my cat's uncontrollable urge to rub against my face at 2 a.m.

Terri L. Haney

August 20

There has never been a cat who couldn't calm me down by walking slowly past my chair.

Rod McKuen

August 21

All children left unattended will be given a free kitten.

Sign in a veterinarian's office

August 22

A dog is like a liberal. He wants to please everybody. A cat doesn't need to know that everybody loves him.

William Kunstler

August 23

Life is hard. Soften yours with a cat.
Unknown

August 24

A little drowsing cat is an image of perfect beatitude.

Jules Champfleury

August 25

I have found my love of cats most helpful in understanding women.

John Simon

August 26

The trouble with cats is that they've got no tact.

P. G. Wodehouse

August 27

I had been told that the training procedure with cats was difficult. It's not. Mine had me trained in two days.

Bill Dana

August 28

Cats do not have to be shown how to have a good time, for they are unfailingly ingenious in that respect.

James Mason

August 29

Women, poets, and especially artists, like cats; delicate natures only can realize their sensitive nervous systems.

Helen M. Winslow

August 30

Few people are mugwumps about the cat.

William H. A. Carr

August 31

There are no ordinary cats.
Colette

September 1

To kill a cat brings seventeen years of bad luck.

Irish Proverb

September 2

Two things are aesthetically perfect in the world—the clock and the cat.

Emile Auguste Chartier

September 3

If you want to know the character of
a man, find out what his
cat thinks of him.

Unknown

September 4

You'll never need a lawn ornament if you have a cat in the yard.

Katherine Palmer Peterson

September 5

The cat Bastet sat perched on the rim of the tub, watching me through slitted golden eyes. She was fascinated by baths. I suppose total immersion in water must have seemed to her a peculiar method of cleansing oneself.

Elizabeth Peters

September 6

In the matter of animals, I love only cats, but I love them unreasonably for their qualities and in spite of their numerous faults. I have only one, but I could not live without a cat.

J. K. Huysmans

September 7

Sometimes he sits at your feet looking into your face with an expression so gentle and caressing that the depth of this gaze startles you.

Theophile Gautier

September 8

Cats do not declare their love much; they enact it, by their myriad invocations of our pleasure.

Vicki Hearne

September 9

To escort a cat on a leash is against the nature of the cat.

Adlai Stevenson

September 10

The cat always leaves a mark
on his friend.
Spanish Proverb

September 11

Cats are so unpredictable. You just never know how they'll ignore you next.

Unknown

September 12

She knows that nine lives
are enough.
Oswald Barron

September 13

That cat will write her autograph all over your leg if you let her.

Mark Twain

September 14

Some people say that cats are sneaky, evil, and cruel. True, and they have many other fine qualities as well.

Missy Dizick

September 15

A cat stretches from one end of my childhood to the other.

Blaga Dimitrova

September 16

But ask the animals, and they will teach you, or the birds of the air, and they will tell you.

Job 12:7

September 17

The cat is magical and the bringer of good luck.

Indian Proverb

September 18

Cats are forever.

François Fossier

September 19

A cat has absolute emotional honesty; human beings, for one reason or another, may hide their feelings, but a cat does not.

Robert Herrick

September 20

Cats hate water only when it is dumped on them, as who wouldn't? Given the opportunity, they will fish diligently in the neighborhood fish ponds.

Eric Temple Bell

September 21

If a cat can detect no self-advantage in what it is being told to do, it says the hell with it, and, if pressure is brought to bear, it will grow increasingly surly and irritable to the point where it is hopeless to continue.

John D. MacDonald

September 22

Some people say man is the most dangerous animal on the planet. Obviously those people have never met an angry cat.

Lillian Johnson

September 23

A dog is a dog, a bird is a bird, and a cat is a person.

Mugsy Peabody

September 24

Cats do not go for a walk to get somewhere but to explore.

Sidney Denham

September 25

Some people own cats and go on to lead normal lives.

Unknown

September 26

The phrase "domestic cat" is an oxymoron.

George F. Will

September 27

The cat is a wild animal that inhabits the homes of humans.

Konrad Lorenz

September 28

If you want to be a psychological novelist and write about human beings, the best thing you can do is keep a pair of cats.

Aldous Huxley

September 29

Even overweight, cats instinctively know the cardinal rule: When fat, arrange yourself in slim poses.

John Weitz

September 30

Nature breaks through the eyes of the cat.

Irish Proverb

October 1

Cats are the ultimate narcissists. You can tell this by all the time they spend on personal grooming. Dogs aren't like this. A dog's idea of personal grooming is to roll in a dead fish.

James Gorman

October 2

A cat determined not to be found can fold itself up like a pocket handkerchief if it wants to.

Dr. Louis J. Camuti

October 3

My cat does not talk as respectfully to me as I do to her.

Colette

October 4

Way down deep, we're all motivated by the same urges. Cats have the courage to live by them.
Jim Davis

October 5

When moving to a new home, always put the cat through the window instead of the door, so that it will not leave.

American Proverb

October 6

Everything that moves, serves to interest and amuse a cat. He is convinced that nature is busying herself with his diversion; he can conceive of no other purpose in the universe.

F. A. Paradis de Moncrif

October 7

That cat that has its mouth burned by drinking hot milk will not drink even buttermilk without first blowing upon it.

Indian Proverb

October 8

Meow is like aloha—
it can mean anything.

Hank Ketchum

October 9

They purr to signal a relaxed mood, and their purring may also help relax them and those around them who feel and hear their purring—like getting a nice massage in sound.

Michael W. Fox, DVM

October 10

It was difficult to feel vexed by a creature that burst into a chorus of purring as soon as I spoke to him.
Philip Brown

October 11

Nature abhors a vacuum, but not as much as cats do.

Lee Entrekin

October 12

If a cat spoke, it would say things like, "Hey, I don't see the problem here."

Roy Blount Jr.

October 13

The King will reply, "I tell you the truth, whatever you did for one of the least of these brothers of mine, you did for me."

Matthew 25:40

October 14

If stretching were wealth, the cat would be rich.

African Proverb

October 15

Some cats is blind,
and stone-deaf some,
but ain't no cat
wuz ever dumb.

Anthony Henderson Euwer

October 16

The cat is the animal to whom the Creator gave the biggest eye, the softest fur, the most supremely delicate nostrils, a mobile ear, an unrivaled paw, and a curved claw borrowed from the rose-tree.

Colette

October 17

Cats have always been associated with the Moon. Like the Moon, they come to life at night, escaping from humanity and wandering over housetops with their eyes beaming out through the darkness.
Patricia Dale-Green

October 18

Cats may sense early on that you don't like paw prints on your butter, but they will jump onto any surface in the home as long as no one sees it happen.

Kathy Young

October 19

Kittens can happen to anyone.
Paul Gallico

October 20

You own a dog; you feed a cat.
Jim Fiebig

October 21

A cat which is kept as a household pet may properly be considered a thing of value. It ministers to the pleasures of its owner and serves with honor.

Unknown

October 22

The cat seldom interferes with other people's rights. His intelligence keeps him from doing many of the fool things that complicate life.

Carl van Vechten

October 23

A cat, though independent, has a way of letting you know that without you, life just wouldn't be worthwhile.

Sharon Lundblad

October 24

All cats love fish but fear to wet their paws.
Chinese Proverb

October 25

The mathematical probability of a common cat doing exactly as it pleases is the one scientific absolute in the world.

Lynn M. Osband

October 26

Cats were put into the world to disprove the dogma that all things were created to serve man.

Paul Gray

October 27

A kitten is a rosebud in the garden of the animal kingdom.

Robert Southey

October 28

A rose has thorns; a cat has claws. Certainly both are worth the risk.

Unknown

October 29

If there is one spot of sun spilling onto the floor, a cat will find it and soak it up.

Jean Asper-McIntosh

October 30

A cat is never a presentation,
but an innocent happening.
Alwin Nikolais

October 31

A cat isn't fussy—just so long as you remember he likes his milk in the shallow, rose-patterned saucer and his fish on the blue plate. From which he will take it, and eat it off the floor.

Arthur Bridges

November 1

Most of us rather like our cats to have a streak of wickedness. I should not feel quite easy in the company of any cat that walked about the house with a saintly expression.

Beverly Nichols

November 2

After extensive research, I have determined that cats do have nine lives. But this has made for some awkward moments on the autopsy table since you can never really tell which life is nine.
David James

November 3

... Supposing you're trying to find out how a cat works—you take that cat apart to see how it works, what you've got in your hands is a non-working cat. The cat wasn't a sort of ... mechanism that was susceptible to our available tools of analysis.

Douglas Adams

November 4

With the qualities of cleanliness, affection, patience, dignity, and courage that cats have, how many of us, I ask you, would be capable of becoming cats?

Fernand Mery

November 5

People who hate cats will come back as mice in their next life.

Faith Resnick

November 6

I have noticed that what cats most appreciate in a human being is not the ability to produce food which they take for granted—but his or her entertainment value.

Geoffrey Household

November 7

Give a cat a fish, and you feed her for a day; teach a cat to fish, and she will wait for you to feed her.

H. B. S.

November 8

If left to their own devices, felines tend to nap and nibble throughout the day and night, scarcely differentiating between the two.

Lynn Hollyn

November 9

> The real objection to the great majority of cats is their insufferable air of superiority.
>
> **P. G. Wodehouse**

November 10

Now, as you all know, there is nothing a cat dislikes so much as water; just watch your kitty shake her paws daintily when she steps into a puddle, and see how disgusted she is if a drop of water falls on her nose and back.

Agnes A. Sandham

November 11

A computer and a cat are somewhat alike—they both purr, and like to be stroked, and spend a lot of the day motionless. They also have secrets they don't necessarily share.

John Updike

November 12

If I called her, she would pretend not to hear, but would come a few moments later when it could appear that she had thought of doing so first.

Arthur Weigall

November 13

There is something about the presence of a cat... that seems to take the bite out of being alone.

Dr. Louis J. Camuti

November 14

Cats always land on their feet. Dogs won't even let you throw them.

Unknown

November 15

Cats are peaceful and tranquil—they bring calmness with their serene personalities.

Chris Evert

November 16

Your righteousness is like the mighty mountains, your justice like the great deep. O Lord, you preserve both man and beast.

Psalm 36:6

November 17

When you're special to a cat, you're special indeed—she brings to you the gift of her preference of you, the sight of you, the sound of your voice, the touch of your hand.

Lenore Fleischer

November 18

One can pick a cat to fit almost any kind of decor, color scheme, income, personality, mood. But under the fur, whatever color it may be, there still lies, essentially unchanged, one of the world's free souls.

Eric Gurney

November 19

He will be your friend, if he finds you worthy of friendship, but not your slave.... but if he once gives himself to you, it is with absolute confidence and fidelity of affection. God has created the cat to give man the pleasure of caressing the tiger.

Theophile Gautier

November 20

Purring would seem to be, in her case, an automatic safety valve device for dealing with happiness overflow.

Monica Edwards

November 21

Cats always know whether people like or dislike them. They do not always care enough to do anything about it.

Winifred Carriere

November 22

I love cats, I adore cats, and may be forgiven for putting one in the sky, after sixty years of hard work.

J. J. L. de Lalande,
on his efforts to launch
a cat into space

November 23

I named my kitten Rose—fur soft as a petal, claws sharper than thorns.

Astrid Alauda

November 24

A cat can purr its way out of anything.

Donna McCrohan

November 25

Even the stupidest cat seems to know more than any dog.

Eleanor Clark

November 26

Cats can derive their nutrition from the air they breathe until you get the message that the Fish Fin Buffet you put in their bowl three days ago will never be acceptable.

Kathy Young

November 27

The cat has nine lives—three for playing, three for straying, and three for staying.

English Proverb

November 28

Your cat will never threaten your popularity by barking at three in the morning. He won't attack the mailman or eat the drapes, although he may climb the drapes to see how the room looks from the ceiling.

Helen Powers

November 29

Cats are cool. They have style, personality, sophistication, and just the right amount of confidence.

Michael Bolton

November 30

A house without a dog or a cat is the house of a scoundrel.

Portuguese Proverb

December 1

Owning a cat is a good forerunner of marriage. You learn that you cannot control another living being, or expect him/her to do everything you want.

Unknown

December 2

If a cat did not put a firm paw down now and then, how could his human remain possessed?

Winifred Carriere

December 3

A cat cares for you only as a source of food, security, and a place in the sun. Her high self-sufficiency is her charm.

Charles Horton Cooley

December 4

The great charm of cats is their rampant egotism, their devil-may-care attitude toward responsibility, their disinclination to earn an honest dollar... cats are disdainful of everything but their own immediate interests.

Robertson Davies

December 5

No one can have experienced to the fullest the true sense of achievement and satisfaction who has never pursued and successfully caught his tail.

Rosalind Welcher

December 6

I love cats. I love their grace and their elegance. I love their independence and their arrogance, and the way they lie and look at you, summing you up, surely to your detriment, with that unnerving, unwinking, appraising stare.

Joyce Stranger

December 7

There are people who reshape the world by force or argument, but the cat just lies there, dozing, and the world quietly reshapes itself to suit his comfort and convenience.

Ivy Dodd

December 8

A creature that never cries over spilt milk: a cat.
Evan Esar

December 9

Happiness does not light gently on my shoulder like a butterfly. She pounces on my lap, demanding that I scratch behind her ears.

Unknown

December 10

A cat will sit washing his face within two inches of a dog in the most frantic state of barking rage, if the dog be chained.

Carl van Vechten

December 11

Of all animals, the cat alone attains to the contemplative life. He regards the wheel of existence from without, like the Buddha.
Andrew Lang

December 12

Looking at a cat, like looking at clouds or stars or the ocean, makes it difficult to believe there is nothing miraculous in this world.

Leonard Michaels

December 13

Cats keep their cool, no matter what. Even when they do things like fall or lose their balance, they'll walk away with an attitude that seems to say, "I meant to do that."

Michael Jordan

December 14

If you stared deep into a cat's eyes, you would be able to see into the world of spirits.

British Proverb

December 15

The smallest feline is a masterpiece.

Leonardo da Vinci

December 16

A cat is a puzzle for which there is no solution.

Hazel Nicholson

December 17

No Heaven will ever Heaven be unless my cats are there to welcome me.

Unknown

December 18

The cat lives alone. He has no need of society. He obeys only when he wishes, he pretends to sleep the better to see, and scratches everything he can scratch.

Francois Rene de Chateaubriand

December 19

Most cats, when they are Out want to be In, and vice versa, and often simultaneously.

Dr. Louis J. Camuti

December 20

A meow massages the heart.
Stuart McMillan

December 21

No other animal inspires such devotion as the cat.

Linda Sunshine

December 22

Cats are a mysterious kind of folk. There is more passing in their minds than we are aware of.

Sir Walter Scott

December 23

Life is hard, then you nap.

Unknown

December 24

If cats seem distant and aloof, it is because this is not their native planet—they are here just to visit and dominate.

Hank Roll

December 25

If there were to be a universal sound depicting peace, I would surely vote for the purr.

Barbara Diamond

December 26

Since each of us is blessed with only one life, why not live it with a cat?

Robert Stearns

December 27

I cannot exist without a cat.... Life would not be worth living without a cat.

Peggy Bacon

December 28

For purring beside our fireplaces and pattering along our back fences, we have got a wild beast as uncowed and uncorrupted as any under heaven.

Alan Devoe

December 29

The thing about cats, as you may find, is that no one knows what they have in mind.

John Ciardi

December 30

Cats are independent, but completely loyal friends for life.

Anthony Edwards

December 31

Cats' whiskers are so sensitive, they can find their way through the narrowest crack in a broken heart.

Unknown